From flaw to flow

A Practical Guide to unlock Hidden talents and Improve Flow

By: Eduardo J. Estrada

From Flaw to Flow

Eduardo J. Estrada

Published by Eduardo J. Estrada, 2023.

While every precaution has been taken in the preparation of this book, the publisher assumes no responsibility for errors or omissions, or for damages resulting from the use of the information contained herein.

FROM FLAW TO FLOW

First edition. July 1, 2023.

ISBN: 979-8223718468

Written by Eduardo J. Estrada.

Table of Contents

Introduction 1

PART I: The Problem with Ignoring Unused Talent............................3

Chapter 1: The 8th Lean Waste - Skill or Unused Talent 5

Chapter 2: Grow to Flow - A Focus in Lean.................................. 11

PART II: Empowering Companies to Utilize Unused Talent........ 19

Chapter 3: Companies are Groups of People..................................... 21

Chapter 4: Giving Voice and Listening Time to your Team 31

PART III: Embracing Flaws and Letting Them Glow...................... 39

Chapter 5: Fuelling Motivation with the Correct Tools.................. 41

Chapter 6: Let Them Glow - Embracing Flaws............................ 49

Conclusion... 57

References 59

Acknowledgments.. 63

This Book is dedicated to my Family and All great Talents that are improving our world every day.

Introduction

Every person has a unique set of skills, talents, and experiences that they bring into the workplace or any project. Unfortunately, many of these talents go unnoticed, leading to missed opportunities for personal and organizational improvement. In today's business environment, companies and countries are constantly searching for ways to improve their efficiency and customer experience. However, they often overlook one of their most valuable resources - their own people.

During my professional experience I have noticed the traditional management approaches and embraced the power of diverse perspectives from colleagues, managers, and team members. There is so much creativity and true potential in the workforce, but sometimes either due to the vague role descriptions, people's mindset or simply managers not noticing, all that potential goes to waste.

In this book, my aim is to condense and explore some of the already tested Lean Manufacturing concepts and relate them to improve the utilization of unused talents in the workplace. We will examine the 8th Lean Waste, referred to "Skill or Unused Talent" and how it contributes to inefficiency and waste in companies. By identifying and utilizing these talents, companies can move from a finding flaws culture into a more streamlined and effective work environment, while also enhancing customer and staff experience.

Part 1 of this book will focus on the problem with ignoring unused talent in the workplace. Chapter 1 will define the 8th Lean Waste and its impact on companies. Chapter 2 will examine the principles of Lean and how incorporating unused talent into Lean processes can lead to increased efficiency and profitability.

Part 2 of the book will focus on empowering staff to utilize their unused talents. Chapter 3 will explore the importance of company culture in promoting the utilization of unused talent. Chapter 4 will discuss the importance of creating open channels of communication between staff and management.

Finally, in Part 3, we will discuss the importance of embracing flaws and letting them glow. Chapter 5 will examine the role of technology in unlocking employee talent. Chapter 6 will examine the benefits of creating a culture that encourages experimentation and learning from failures. By embracing imperfection, companies can also create an environment that encourages personal and organizational growth.

By embracing unused talent and flaws, you can create a more efficient, innovative, and profitable workplace. This book aims to provide practical strategies for identifying and utilizing employee talent and will demonstrate how companies can create a culture that encourages personal and organizational growth.

It will be great to hear about your journey, your learnings and even better your improved Team Experience.

PART I: The Problem with Ignoring Unused Talent

In this section, we will be exploring the concept of unused talent is the eighth lean waste, a term coined by the Lean manufacturing philosophy. Companies that ignore this waste, which involves not utilizing the skills and knowledge of their staff, not only harm their own growth but also negatively impact the customer experience. By neglecting to leverage the abilities of their team members, businesses miss out on opportunities to improve their processes and better serve their customers.

The detrimental effects that occur when a company fails to identify, develop, and utilize the talents of its team members and staff not given the opportunity to explore their full potential, results in a loss of valuable resources and growth.

In this section, we will explore into the causes and consequences of ignoring unused talent. We will discuss the cultural and systemic factors that contribute to this issue and provide real-life examples of companies that have struggled with unused talent. Additionally, we will explore the benefits that businesses can reap from identifying and harnessing their staff talents, including increased productivity, improved job satisfaction, and enhanced customer experience.

By the end of Part 1, the aim is that you will have a thorough understanding of the importance of addressing the eighth lean waste and the costs of ignoring unused talent. We hope this section will inspire individuals and companies to reassess their approach to talent management and create a more inclusive and productive work environment.

Chapter 1: The 8th Lean Waste - Skill or Unused Talent

"The person born with a talent they are meant to use will find their greatest happiness in using it." - Johann Wolfgang von Goethe

Defining the 8th Lean Waste and how it affects companies?

Part of the first definitions of Lean waste didn't include the use of the great business resource of skills and talents, which was often overlooked in traditional Lean methodologies.

The 8th Lean Waste refers to the underutilization of employee skills, talents, and knowledge. It is also known as Skill wastage or Unused Talent, which refers to the untapped potential that exists within a company's workforce.

The impact that wasted talent can have on a company's bottom line is tremendous if not addressed on time, this can be just as detrimental to a company's success as any of the other seven Lean wastes.

This waste occurs when employees are not given the opportunity to use their full potential, or when their skills are not aligned with the needs of the company. A Skill waste can manifest itself in various ways, such as employee disengagement, low morale, and turnover.

The impact of the 8th Lean Waste on a company can be significant. When employees are not given the opportunity to utilize their full potential, they become disengaged and demotivated. This can lead to decreased productivity, increased errors, and ultimately, decreased profits.

Additionally, when employees feel undervalued or underutilized, they may look for opportunities elsewhere, leading to high turnover rates.

According to study by Gallup (Gallup, 2022), only 13% of employees are engaged in their work, which means that 87% of workers could be disengaged. When employees feel undervalued or underutilized, they may become disengaged and apathetic, leading to decreased motivation and productivity. This can create a cycle of disengagement that is difficult to break, as employees may begin to feel that their efforts are not valued or appreciated.

The 8th Lean Waste can also have a negative impact on the customer experience. When employees are not able to use their full potential, they may be unable to provide the level of service that customers expect. This can lead to decreased customer satisfaction and ultimately, lost business.

The impact of the 8th Lean Waste on a company is significant for several reasons. First and foremost, companies that do not utilize the full potential of their staff will inevitably experience decreased productivity and efficiency. This can lead to missed deadlines, increased errors, and a general sense of disorganization that can be felt throughout the organization. In turn, these issues can negatively impact the company's reputation and its ability to compete in the marketplace.

The impact of the 8th Lean Waste extends beyond the walls of the company itself. When employees are not able to utilize their full potential, it can negatively impact the customer experience. Customers expect high levels of service and support, and when employees are not able to provide this due to a lack of training, resources, or motivation, it can lead to decreased customer satisfaction and ultimately, lost business. This can have a ripple effect throughout the industry, as dissatisfied customers may choose to take their business elsewhere, ultimately harming the company's reputation and bottom line.

Addressing the 8th Lean Waste requires a shift in mindset from traditional Lean methodologies. Companies must recognize the value of their employees' skills and talents to make a concerted effort to align these with the needs of the business.

This may involve providing training and development opportunities, creating cross-functional teams, or implementing job rotations to allow employees to gain new skills and experiences.

The importance of identifying and utilizing unused talents and skills in employees

THE 8TH LEAN WASTE - Skill or Unused Talent - is a significant waste that can have a detrimental impact on your company's bottom line. One of the primary reasons why the 8th Lean Waste is so detrimental to a company is that it represents a lost opportunity for growth and improvement.

When employees are not given the opportunity to utilize their full potential, the company misses out on the unique skills and knowledge that everyone brings to the table.

By recognizing the value of employee skills and talents and making a concerted effort to address this waste, a business can create a more engaged, motivated, and productive workforce, leading to increased profits and a better customer experience.

The first step in addressing the 8th Lean Waste is to identify the unused talents and skills that exist within the workforce. This can be done through a variety of methods, such as conducting skills assessments, performance evaluations, and employee surveys. It is important to create an environment where employees feel comfortable sharing their skills and experiences, as this can help to uncover hidden talents and knowledge.

One way to identify opportunities is using a so-called Lean Audit, which is only a series of questions to uncover any of the eight lean wastes. Some examples of questions to uncover the 8th lean waste in your business or section could be:

- Are staff being utilized effectively?
- Are staff members being cross-trained?
- Are we utilizing the full potential of our workforce?
- Are we providing training and development opportunities?

Once the unused talents and skills have been identified, it is important to create opportunities for employees to utilize them. This may involve providing additional training and development opportunities, creating cross-functional teams, or assigning special projects that align with an employee's unique skillset. It is also important to ensure that staff have the necessary resources and support to succeed in utilizing their unused talents and skills.

The importance of utilizing unused talents and skills is numerous. When staff are given the opportunity to utilize their full potential, they become more engaged, motivated, and productive. This can lead to increased innovation, improved efficiency, and ultimately, increased profits. Additionally, when staff feels valued and supported, they are more likely to stay with your company long-term, reducing turnover rates and associated costs.

As Johann Wolfgang von Goethe said, "The person born with a talent they are meant to use will find their greatest happiness in using it." By tapping into the talents and potential of staff, businesses can create a happier and more fulfilling work environment for everyone.

Talent that plays small does not serve the world

A BEAUTIFUL PASSAGE from Marianne Williamson's book, Return to Love, (Williamson, n.d.) shows the importance of using our talents to their fullest potential. This quote can be related to the eighth lean waste of unused skill.

Marianne says that "Our deepest fear is not that we are inadequate. Our deepest fear is that we are powerful beyond measure. It is our light, not our darkness that most frightens us. We ask ourselves, 'Who am I to be brilliant, gorgeous, talented, fabulous?' Actually, who are you not to be? You are a child of God. Your playing small does not serve the world. There is nothing enlightened about shrinking so that other people won't feel insecure around you. We are all meant to shine, as children do. We were born to make manifest the glory of God that is within us. It's not just in some of us; it's in everyone. And as we let our own light shine, we unconsciously give other people permission to do the same. As we are liberated from our own fear, our presence automatically liberates others."

As the eighth lean waste refers to the underutilization of people's skills and abilities, I wanted to include this quote as a reminder that we should give others and ourselves the opportunity to use talents, to achieve engagement, improve productivity, quality, and innovation.

When people are not given the chance to use their abilities, it is not only unhelpful to their team or organisation, but also to themselves. People who are not challenged or interested in their work may grow dissatisfied with their employment or projects, resulting in lower job satisfaction, motivation, and retention. This can lead to a high turnover rate, greater recruiting and training expenses, and a loss of institutional expertise.

To solve the eighth lean waste, organisations must focus on maximising worker talents and competencies. This may be accomplished by giving employees with chances for training and growth, including them in decision-making processes, fostering creativity, and allocating duties that are aligned with their talents and abilities. In addition to improving organizational performance, utilizing employees' talents can have a positive impact on the society.

By allowing your team and staff to use their talents, your organization can create new products and services that easily improve people's lives, solve big society challenges, and drive economic growth.

Chapter Summary/Key Takeaways

- Addressing the 8th Lean Waste requires a shift in mindset and a commitment to valuing and supporting staff, but the potential benefits are significant and far-reaching.
- By identifying and utilizing talents, companies can create a more engaged, motivated, and productive workforce, leading to increased innovation, improved efficiency, and ultimately, increased profits.
- Addressing the 8th Lean Waste is not only a way to improve the bottom line, but also a way to create a positive and supportive workplace culture that benefits both employees and your company.
-

Chapter 2: Grow to Flow - A Focus in Lean

"When I stand before God at the end of my life, I would hope that I would not have a single bit of talent left, and could say, 'I used everything you gave me." - Erma Bombeck.

The ability to pick up new skills and adjust to shifting business conditions is essential for success, thus investing in the skill development of your team will undoubtedly improve your prospects of success and competitiveness.

Encouraging your staff and team to take on new challenges, grow in their professions, and learn new skills will keep them imaginative and creative.

When your team members are given the opportunity to develop their skills and grow in their careers, they are more likely to be engaged and committed to their work. A report (Linkedin, 2018) found that 94% of employees would stay with a company longer if it invested in their career development.

If your staff are better equipped to meet the needs of customers, then it will naturally result in higher levels of customer satisfaction. A study by Gallup (Gallup, State of the Global Workplace Report, 2022) found that organizations with high levels of employee engagement have 10% higher customer ratings and 20% higher sales than those with low levels of engagement.

In this chapter, we will explore the benefits of developing skills in the workforce so they can Glow and deliver results. Developing the skills of your workforce will surely help you to stay competitive in the marketplace.

By investing in employee training and development, organizations can unlock the untapped talent of their workforce, driving success and achieving their goals. From improved productivity to enhanced customer satisfaction and a competitive advantage, the benefits of skill development are clear. As the world continues to evolve, organizations and people must prioritize skill development to stay ahead of the curve and remain competitive.

Understanding the principles of Lean and its relationship with unused talent

ACCORDING TO THE LEAN philosophy, "Value" is any action or process that the customer pays for and is willing to pay. "Waste" can also be defined as anything in your operation that doesn't add value to the customer.

One of the most suitable definitions of Lean that I find mainly relevant is by Mr. John Shook, who said that "Lean is a philosophy which shortens the time between the customer order and the product build/shipment by eliminating sources of waste."

In today's business climate, offering excellent client experience is essential for any organisation's success. However, providing excellent customer service can be difficult, especially when waste occurs in the process.

It is critical to find flow and eliminate waste in any process to enhance customer experience. A relevant tool that you can use to minimise unused talent in operations is a Lean Waste Audit which contains eight different kinds of wastes. This tool is normally based in the TIM WOODS framework.

The TIM WOODS framework is an acronym that has been used as part of the Waste Audit tools in lean management, to identify and eliminate waste in processes.

The acronym stands for:

- Transport
- Inventory
- Motion
- Waiting
- Overproduction
- Overprocessing
- Defects
- Skills or unused Talent

By identifying and eliminating waste in each of these areas, you can streamline your business processes and improve the efficiency and effectiveness of customer experience. Let's see some basic definitions.

Transport: this waste occurs when unnecessary movement of people or products is required. In the any process, this can include unnecessary transfers of information or equipment between departments. For example, to reduce transport waste in customer service, organizations can use tools such as value stream mapping to identify areas where transportation can be reduced or eliminated.

Inventory: this waste occurs when more inventory is produced or maintained than is needed. An example for a customer service process can include excessive inventory of customer data or equipment. To reduce inventory waste, you can use tools such as just-in-time (JIT) production to produce only what is needed when it is needed.

Motion: this waste occurs when unnecessary movement of people or equipment is required. In the service process, this can include excessive movement to make a simple cup of coffee while serving a customer or passing customer data between departments. To reduce motion waste in your operations, you can use tools such as the Spaghetti Diagram or 6S (Sort, Set in Order, Shine, Standardize, Sustain and Safety) to improve workplace organization and reduce unnecessary movement.

Waiting: this waste occurs when time is wasted waiting for a process to complete. In a process, this can include waiting for customer data or equipment to be processed. To reduce waiting waste in customer service, organizations can use tools such as Kanban to manage inventory levels and production schedules, reducing the need for customers to wait for products to be produced.

Overproduction: this waste occurs when more products or services are produced than is needed. In the customer service process, this can include producing too much food or too much data or widgets. To reduce overproduction waste, you can use tools such as flow production to produce only what is needed when it is needed.

Overprocessing: this waste occurs when more work is done than is needed to produce a product or service. In the customer service process, this can include performing unnecessary tasks or using overly complex systems to process customer data or equipment. To reduce overprocessing waste, you can use tools such as value stream mapping to identify areas where overprocessing can be reduced or eliminated.

Defects: this waste occurs when errors or defects are produced in the production process. In the customer service process, this can include incorrect customer orders or incorrect service delivery. To reduce defect waste, you can use tools such as mistake-proofing to prevent errors from occurring in the first place.

Skills: this waste occurs when employees are not fully utilised, or their skills are not being improved effectively. In your service or process, this can include underutilizing the skills of customer service representatives. To improve skills, you can use tools such as coaching, training, job rotation to cross-train employees, improving their skills and making them more versatile in their roles.

Some other key principles from Lean Manufacturing, include the continuous improvement, waste reduction and value stream mapping, which can be easily applied to improvement of Staff and Customer experience.

Many companies discovered a strong link between greater productivity and better quality during the development of Lean and

Quality management, implying that having best-in-class quality does not necessitate additional effort; in fact, companies with the greatest productivity were also the best in quality.

The benefits of incorporating unused talent into Lean processes

INCORPORATING UNUSED talent into Lean processes is a key component of creating a more efficient and effective workplace. By identifying the skills and knowledge that exist within your workforce, you can better leverage these resources to improve processes, reduce waste, and increase overall productivity.

One of the primary benefits of incorporating unused talent into Lean processes is the ability to reduce waste. When staff can utilize their unique skills and knowledge, they can help identify inefficiencies in the current process and suggest improvements. This can lead to a reduction in waste, whether it be in the form of excess inventory, overproduction, or unnecessary motion.

In addition to reducing waste, incorporating unused talent into lean processes can also lead to increased innovation. When staff are encouraged to think creatively and share their ideas, they may be able to identify new and innovative solutions to existing problems. This helps to increase your competitive advantage in the marketplace, as companies that can innovate and adapt quickly are more likely to succeed in the long run.

Incorporating unused talent into lean processes can lead to a more engaged and motivated workforce. When staff feel valued and supported, they are more likely to be invested in the success of the company. This can lead to increased productivity, reduced absenteeism, and improved overall job satisfaction.

According to the 2020 report by Gallup (Gallup, State of the Global Workplace Report, 2022), the researchers took 11 performance metrics and compared them between the companies with the higher and lower levels of engagement, the results showed the following differences in business outcomes:

- 81% in absenteeism
- 58% in patient safety incidents (mortality and falls)
- 18% in turnover for high-turnover organizations
- 43% in turnover for low-turnover organizations
- 28% in shrinkage (theft)
- 64% in safety incidents (accidents)
- 41% in quality (defects)
- 10% in customer loyalty/engagement
- 18% in productivity (sales)
- 23% in profitability

This shows how critical it is to have staff fully trained and engaged in the processes.

To achieve higher levels of engagement, companies require a shift in mindset and a commitment to valuing and supporting employees.

Incorporating unused talent into your processes is a critical component of creating a more efficient and effective workplace. By identifying the skills and knowledge that exist within the workforce and leveraging these resources to improve processes, companies can reduce waste, increase flow, improve innovation, and create a more engaged and motivated workforce.

It is essential to understand the strong link between greater productivity, better quality, and using the talents of your team. By leveraging the skills and abilities of staff, businesses can achieve significant improvements in productivity and quality.

When considering Quality as a measure of how well a product or service meets customer requirements, then using the talents of staff, you can also improve quality in several ways, including:

- Process improvement: Employees with specific skills and

knowledge can contribute to process improvement initiatives, resulting in improved quality.

- Innovation: Employees can use their creativity and problem-solving skills to develop new products and services or improve existing ones, resulting in improved quality.
- Customer Experience: Employees who interact with customers can provide valuable feedback on customer needs and preferences. This feedback can be used to improve product and service quality.

Additional, using the talents of your staff can also lead to improved employee satisfaction and retention, resulting in reduced recruitment and training costs.

Chapter Summary/Key Takeaways

- In a business or project, it is crucial to recognize the importance of employee talents and to invest in their development to achieve long-term success.
- The practical tips outlined in this chapter can help you get started on this journey, but ultimately, it requires a commitment to valuing and supporting staff and a willingness to embrace change and continuous improvement.
- Using the talents of your team is essential to achieve greater productivity and better quality.
- By assigning tasks based on employees' skills and abilities, providing training and development opportunities, engaging employees, and encouraging innovation, you can improve productivity and quality.
-

PART II: Empowering Companies to Utilize Unused Talent

The success of any organization is heavily dependent on the individuals that make up its workforce. At the end companies are groups of people that come together to achieve a common goal. The talent, skills, and expertise of the workforce are what drives the organization forward. However, many companies and organizations fail to recognize and utilize the full potential of their members, resulting in unused talent and lost opportunities.

Companies must understand that their employees are their most valuable asset. They must learn to empower their workforce and provide them with the tools and resources necessary to reach their full potential. By doing so, companies can tap into the unused talent of their employees, increase productivity, and drive growth.

Empowering employees requires a shift in the way companies approach their workforce. It means moving away from a traditional hierarchical structure and embracing a more collaborative and inclusive culture. Employees must be given a voice and be involved in decision-making processes. They should be encouraged to share their ideas and perspectives, and their contributions should be valued and recognized.

By creating a culture that empowers employees, companies can unlock the full potential of their workforce. Employees that feel valued and respected are more likely to be engaged and motivated to perform at their best. They are more willing to take risks and innovate, leading to new ideas and opportunities for the organization. Additionally, by utilizing the full potential of their workforce, companies can better adapt to changing market conditions and stay ahead of the competition.

Chapter 3: Companies are Groups of People

"A great deal of talent is lost to the world for want of a little courage. Every day sends to their graves obscure men whose timidity prevented them from making a first effort." - Sydney Smith.

Considering that Organizations and Companies are groups of people that come together to achieve a common goal, then empowering their members to utilize their talents is key to driving organizational success.

Companies and leaders have the responsibility to create a culture that values and respects their workforce, encourages collaboration and inclusivity, and recognizes the contributions of all members.

The practical tips outlined in this chapter can help you improve culture, but ultimately, it requires a commitment to valuing and supporting employees and a willingness to embrace change and continuous improvement.

The Impact of Company Culture on Unused Talent

I'VE FOUND VERY INTERESTING how Lance Secretan, defines what effective leadership is (SECRETAN, 2004): "Leadership is not so much about technique and methods as it is about opening the heart. Leadership is about inspiration—of oneself and of others. Great leadership is about human experiences, not processes. Leadership is not a formula or a program, it is a human activity that comes from the heart and considers the hearts of others."

In order to foster an environment that encourages the utilization of unused talent, any leader should first recognize that companies are ultimately groups of people. While processes and systems are important, it is the people within an organization that ultimately drive success.

Here we explore how company leaders can create an environment that encourages the utilization of unused talent and provides practical tips for implementing these strategies in the workplace.

A good first step in creating an environment that encourages the utilization of unused talent is recognizing the importance of people in a company or organization. Leaders should acknowledge that the skills and knowledge that exist within their team are critical resources that can help drive success. This means investing in staff development, providing opportunities for cross-functional collaboration, and creating a culture that values and supports their members.

As they say, "A good salary can motivate a person once a month, but a good work culture motivates them every single day".

Fostering an environment where staff is encouraged to share their ideas and suggestions for improving processes and workflows, impacts in the utilization of unused talent while creating a culture of continuous improvement. Leaders should provide the necessary resources and support for employees to implement these ideas and reward successful initiatives.

An environment with diversity and inclusion should be embedded in your organization or project. This includes showing it in policies, procedures, communication and examining how are reflected in the structures of your teams.

Additionally, by creating a culture of continuous improvement, you can tap into the diverse skills and knowledge that exist within your workforce and continuously drive success.

Another way to encourage the utilization of unused talent is by providing opportunities for professional development. This means investing in training and development programs that align with employees' unique skillsets, interests and providing opportunities for cross-functional training and development. Company leaders should also provide opportunities for employees to take on new challenges and responsibilities, which can help to expand their skillsets and provide opportunities for growth and development.

As a leader you can encourage the utilization of unused talent by fostering team engagement and empowerment. This means providing staff and team members with a voice and listening time, encourage teamwork and provide the necessary tools and resources for success. When employees feel valued and supported, they are more likely to be invested in the success of the company and contribute to its growth and development.

Ultimately companies are groups of people, and it is the skills and knowledge that exist within the workforce that ultimately drive success.

By creating an environment that encourages the utilization of unused talent, company leaders can tap into the diverse skills and knowledge that exist within their workforce and drive continuous improvement and growth.

How company leaders can foster an environment that encourages the utilization of unused talent

FOSTERING AN ENVIRONMENT that encourages the utilization of unused talent can be a challenging task for company leaders. However, by implementing the following strategies, you can create a workplace culture that values and supports staff development and empowers team members to utilize their unique skillsets and knowledge.

Encourage Employee Input and Feedback: Find ways to create a culture that encourages open communication and feedback. This can be done by setting up regular meetings with your team, creating suggestion boxes or online feedback forms, encouraging employees to share their ideas and feedback on various aspects of the company's operations. By doing so, leaders can better understand the unique skillsets and knowledge that employees bring to the table and identify ways to incorporate these talents into the company's workflow.

Provide Opportunities for Learning and Development: investments in you and your staff development are more likely to see a positive impact on your business operations. Provide training and development opportunities that align with the unique skillsets and interests of your employees. This can include cross-functional training programs, mentorship opportunities, and providing access to online learning resources. By investing in employee development, company leaders can encourage the utilization of unused talent and help employees to realize their full potential.

Improve your task allocation: Assigning tasks to employees based on their skills and abilities can improve productivity. When employees are working on tasks that they are skilled in, they can complete them more efficiently, resulting in higher productivity.

Create Cross-Functional Teams: By creating cross-functional teams, you can encourage team members to utilize their unique skillsets and work collaboratively with colleagues from different departments. This can help to break down silos within your organization and promote innovation and creativity. By working with colleagues from different departments, team members can gain exposure to different perspectives and approaches to problem-solving, which can ultimately lead to better business outcomes.

Provide Recognition and Rewards: there are many ways to recognize and reward employees who utilize their unused talents to benefit the company. This can be done through performance evaluations, bonuses, or other types of recognition programs. By providing recognition and rewards, company leaders can encourage employees to continue to utilize their unique skillsets and knowledge to drive success.

Offer Coaching and training: these are the essential elements in creating a culture of continuous improvement and engagement. These two solutions together help you develop your staff skills and knowledge necessary to provide exceptional service to customers. This is so essential, that I would expand more how coaching and training can be used to improve Culture.

Coaching is a process that involves providing feedback and guidance to team members to help them improve their skills and performance. Coaching is an essential tool for improving customer experience because it helps everyone understand their strengths and weaknesses and how they can improve their performance. It also helps employees to develop the necessary skills to provide exceptional service to customers.

This should be an ongoing process that takes place regularly. Managers and supervisors should provide regular feedback to employees, highlighting areas where they excel and areas where they need improvement. This feedback should be specific, constructive, and actionable, providing employees with the necessary information and support to improve their performance.

In addition to providing feedback, coaching should also involve setting goals and objectives. This will help employees to focus on their development and track their progress. Managers and supervisors should work with employees to set achievable goals that are aligned with the organization's objectives. Keeping in mind that goals should be specific, measurable, achievable, relevant, and time bound.

Training is another essential tool for improving customer experience. It provides employees with the knowledge and skills necessary to provide exceptional service to customers. Training can be provided in various forms, including classroom training, online training, and on-the-job training.

Effective training programs should be tailored to the specific needs of employees and the organization. They should be designed to help employees understand the organization's products and services, customer needs and expectations, and how to provide exceptional service. They should also provide employees with the necessary skills to handle customer complaints and resolve problems.

Training programs should also be ongoing to ensure that employees are continually developing their skills and knowledge. New employees should receive comprehensive training to help them understand the organization's culture, values, and expectations. Existing employees should also receive regular training to keep them up to date with new products, services, and technologies.

Get approval to set up a training budget and make sure that your team have access to a variety of training opportunities. This could include formal training courses, on-the-job training, and e-learning.

By implementing these strategies, you can create an environment that encourages the utilization of unused talent and helps your team to realize their full potential. However, it is important to note that this process requires a long-term commitment to employee development and a willingness to embrace change and innovation.

Ultimately, companies that value and support their people are more likely to see positive business outcomes and continued growth and success.

Enhancing team dynamics with human talent and technology

BY IMPLEMENTING STRATEGIES that focus on improving your team dynamics through the utilization of human talent and technology you can create an environment that fosters collaboration, innovation, and success.

When improving the use of unused talent, it requires a holistic view, incorporating the strengths and potential of team members while leveraging technological advancements. By doing so, you can enhance their overall performance and achieve sustainable growth.

Besides recognising and appreciating the unique talents and strengths of team members as human beings, encourage open discussions to share their expertise and experiences with the use of technology. This would help you foster an environment of mutual learning and support.

For example, integrating technology and AI tools would help you facilitate communication, collaboration, and productivity within your team. In the last years all teams and companies that embraced technology, overcame geographical limitations, and leveraged the power of digital connectivity to work together seamlessly.

A good way to enhance your team with the use of technology is to promote a continuous learning and skill development for both in their respective areas of expertise and in emerging technologies.

Aim to offer your team training programs and resources that enable your team to stay updated on technological advancements and equip them with the necessary skills to leverage AI and other technological tools effectively.

Implement investment in skill development in project management software, communication platforms, and virtual collaboration tools that streamline workflows, enhance information sharing, and improve efficiency.

This investment in skill development empowers teams to embrace technology, while contributing to improved team dynamics and outcomes.

Also creating opportunities for cross-functional collaboration within your team, will certainly allow individuals from different departments or areas of expertise to work together on projects and initiatives. This collaborative approach encourages knowledge sharing, diverse perspectives, and innovative problem-solving. By breaking down silos and fostering cross-functional collaboration, teams can leverage the collective intelligence of their members and achieve great outcomes.

Some of the new technological tools that still growing in popularity is the use of Artificial Intelligence for Enhanced decision-making. Using these technologies can support data-driven decision-making processes within your team. These analytics tools have proven useful in a team environment because can process large amounts of data, extract meaningful insights, and provide recommendations for improved decision-making.

The most important recommendation to enhance your team dynamics is always encouraging a culture of psychological safety within the team, an environment where members feel comfortable taking risks, sharing ideas, and expressing their opinions without fear of judgment or retribution. This inclusive environment fosters trust, creativity, and collaboration, enabling teams to harness the full potential of each individual and leverage technology effectively.

By integrating some of these strategies, you can create a dynamic and innovative team environment that maximizes the potential of your company or projects while harnessing the benefits of your team talent.

Chapter Summary/Key Takeaways

- Enhancing teams requires a focus on leveraging individual strengths, embracing technology tools, promoting continuous learning, facilitating cross-functional collaboration, harnessing AI for decision-making, and fostering a culture of psychological safety.
- When team members are working on tasks that they are skilled in, they can complete them more efficiently, resulting in higher productivity.
- Developing skills and knowledge is extremely necessary to provide exceptional service to customers. Take in account that the training has to be tailored to the specific needs of employees and your organization and should be ongoing.
- By acknowledging and utilizing the diverse talents within the team, you can leverage individual strengths to enhance overall team performance.
-

Chapter 4: Giving Voice and Listening Time to your Team

"Nothing is more inspiring than a person with seemingly mediocre talent rising against the odds to become a champion by way of hard work, effort, and perseverance toward their goals." - Zig Ziglar.

As a leader of your organization or project, the success of your team depends on the contributions from everyone. That's why you should make it a priority to give your team members a voice and listen to their concerns.

There are many benefits to giving people a voice. First, it helps them to understand their perspectives and challenges. When you know what's important to your staff, you can make better decisions that support their success., it is important to create a culture of open communication.

This means encouraging employees to speak up and to share their ideas, even if they are different from the majority. It also means being willing to listen to feedback, even if it is negative.

In the article about respect for people (James (Jim) Womack, 2021), Jim Womack mentions: "Over time I've come to realize that this problem-solving process is actually the highest form of respect. The manager is saying to the employees that the manager can't solve the problem alone, because the manager isn't close enough to the problem to know the facts. He or she truly respects the employees' knowledge and their dedication to finding the best answer. But the employees can't solve the problem alone either because they are often too close to the problem to see its context and they may refrain from asking tough questions about their own work. Only by showing mutual respect – each for the other and for each other's role – is it possible to solve problems, make work more satisfying, and move organizational performance to an ever-higher level."

The importance of creating an open communication channel between employees and management

THE EFFECTIVENESS OF communication between staff and management is crucial to any organization's success. Communication problems can result in misunderstandings, mistrust, and a general lack of clarity regarding objectives and expectations. This is particularly true when it comes to locating and making use of underutilised talents and skills within an organisation.

As Atul Malikram mentions in his beautiful reflection about Leadership (Malikram, 2020), "A Leader knows that communication solves all problems. Avoidance worsens all problems."

Fostering an atmosphere where all talents and skills are recognised and utilised requires open communication between management and employees. This may entail holding regular meetings with staff members to talk about their interests, qualifications, and objectives as well as holding frequent feedback sessions to help them advance in their positions.

An open communication channel can also aid in the identification of any challenges that may be stopping employees from fully utilising their talents and skills. This can include training challenges, a lack of resources, or even personal biases or beliefs that are restricting their potential.

Furthermore, an open communication channel can aid in the development of trust and transparency inside the organisation. Employees are more inclined to share their ideas and concerns when they believe they can communicate openly and honestly with management, which can assist to generate innovation and enhance overall performance.

Some statistics that support the importance of giving voice and listening time to staff is for example the study by Gallup (Gallup, 2022) which found that employees who feel like they have a voice are more likely to be engaged in their work (70% vs. 29%). Also, a study by McKinsey found that companies with highly engaged employees are 212% more profitable than companies with low engagement.

Creating an open communication channel between employees and management is essential for unlocking the full potential of a company's workforce. By fostering a culture of trust, transparency, and collaboration, businesses can tap into the diverse skills and talents of their employees and achieve greater levels of success.

According to research done by the Google research team, they have found that psychological safety leads to better team results, "for example, among sales teams, those with high psychological safety exceeded their targets by, on average, 17%. In contrast, those with low psychological safety missed their targets by, on average, 19%." (Catalyst, 2016)

Other benefits that you may also noticed of creating an open communication and psychologically safe channel between staff and management include:

- **Increased Employee Engagement:** When employees feel that their voices are heard, they are more likely to be engaged and invested in their work. They are more likely to take ownership of their roles and responsibilities, which can lead to increased productivity and job satisfaction.
- **Improved Decision-Making:** By soliciting feedback and ideas from employees, companies can make more informed decisions. Employees often have unique perspectives and insights into the company's operations, which can help to identify areas for improvement and innovative solutions.
- **Increased Trust:** When employees feel that their concerns are being heard and addressed, they are more likely to trust management and feel valued as members of the team. This can lead to improved morale and a more positive workplace

culture.

- **Innovative companies:** a study by Harvard Business Review found that companies that listen to their employees are 60% more likely to be innovative.

Strategies for giving employees a voice in decision-making processes

Effective communication between employees and management is critical for any organization's success. However, all too frequently, employees believe that their voices are not getting heard, and that management is unresponsive to their concerns.

An effective way to improve is to develop a more engaged and productive workforce by establishing an open communication channel between employees and management.

However, creating an open communication channel between employees and management can be challenging. Some common obstacles include:

- **Lack of Trust:** Employees may be hesitant to share their concerns if they do not trust management to listen and address them. Look for warning signs that your team needs to improve psychological safety.
- **Fear of Repercussions:** Employees may fear retribution for speaking out or sharing their ideas. Fear of asking for or delivering constructive feedback. Also includes hesitance around expressing divergent ideas and asking "silly" questions
- **Time Constraints:** Managers may feel that they do not have the time to listen to employee feedback or address concerns.

To overcome these challenges, you must be committed to creating a culture of open communication and actively work to build trust with the team. This requires ongoing effort and a willingness to be responsive to feedback. While this requires effort and commitment, the benefits are well worth the investment.

Receiving and providing feedback can improve staff skills and performance; it is an essential tool for improving culture and engagement because it helps employees understand their strengths and weaknesses and how they can improve their performance. While offering input, be interactive and show you're listening.

This also helps your teammates to develop the necessary skills to provide exceptional service to customers. This should be an ongoing process that takes place regularly.

Managers and supervisors should provide regular opportunities to employees, highlighting areas where they excel and areas where they need improvement. This feedback should be specific, constructive, and actionable, providing employees with the necessary information and support to improve their performance.

As mentioned before and in addition to providing feedback, coaching should also involve demonstrating engagement. For example, demonstrating to be present and focus on the conversation while closing your laptop or muting your phone during meetings (if possible) or ask questions with the intention of learning from your colleague.

All leaders in the project or organization should be aware of responding verbally to show engagement and always check your body language; make sure to lean towards or face the person speaking, make eye contact to show connection and active listening.

Engaging employees in decision-making processes and providing a positive work environment can improve their motivation and morale. This can lead to increased productivity and improved quality.

Creating an open communication channel between staff and management requires a good effort on the part of the company's leadership. Some proposed strategies that I have seen working well include:

- Regular Check-Ins: Managers or Supervisors should schedule regular check-ins with their teams to discuss their work, solicit feedback, and address any concerns or challenges. In some cases, they are called Stand Up or Toolbox meetings.
- Anonymous Feedback Mechanisms: you can create anonymous feedback mechanisms, such as suggestion boxes or online surveys, to encourage employees to share their ideas and concerns without fear of retribution. Solicit input, opinions, and feedback from your team.
- Open-Door Policy: all leaders, including Managers and Supervisors should maintain an open-door policy, making themselves available to employees who need to discuss concerns or ideas.
- Weekly What's up meetings: in this case anyone in the organization can announce their updates for the rest of the team, from fundraising activities, team building events, informal announcements, etc. Also, you can keep it open so anyone can be a moderator or presenter. Just try to keep it under 15-20 min per week.
- Town Hall Meetings: this is a bit more formal but can provide updates on company operations and strategy and give employees an opportunity to ask questions, be inclusive in decision-making and provide feedback.
- Be excited when they succeed: When a team or team member reaches an important milestone like getting a promotion, making a first sale, achieving a great result, celebrate it. Some ideas include sending them a Thank you card, telling them how proud you of them are or inviting them to Lunch.
- Being thrilled on someone's behalf: Winning is better when shared. Encourage a positive attitude towards failure by celebrating efforts, even if they result in setbacks. Recognise and reward employees who take risks, learn from their

mistakes, and implement lessons into future ideas.

All the above can help you creating a culture of continuous improvement that encourages staff to stay engaged, share their ideas and suggestions

Giving voice and listening time to staff is not always easy, but it is worth it. When staff feel like they have a voice, they are more likely to be engaged and productive. They are also more likely to come up with new ideas and solutions that can help the organization improve.

Chapter Summary/Key Takeaways

- Creating an open communication channel between employees and leaders is essential for the success of any organization.
- By soliciting feedback and ideas from employees, companies can make more informed decisions, increase employee engagement, and build a culture of trust and transparency.
- Starting with an Open-Door Policy or transparent feedback can help leaders, Managers and Supervisors improving culture and tapping in the unused talents of their team.
-

PART III: Embracing Flaws and Letting Them Glow

While society often places a high value on perfection, the reality is that no one is perfect, and striving for perfection can lead to stress, anxiety, and dissatisfaction.

This section of the book will explore the concept of accepting and embracing imperfection in ourselves and others, also will review the benefits of embracing flaws, including increased self-acceptance, improved relationships, and enhanced creativity. It will also provide practical tips and strategies for using and learning from the imperfection in ourselves and others.

As James Clear mentions "The best way to change the world is in concentric circles: start with yourself and work your way out from there".

By learning to embrace flaws and accept imperfection, team members can develop a more positive and resilient mindset, leading to improved productivity and a more fulfilling team culture.

Overall, "Embracing Flaws and Letting Them Glow" offers a perspective on the importance of imperfection and self-acceptance. By embracing our flaws and letting them shine, we can cultivate a deeper sense of learning, self-awareness, authenticity, and connection with ourselves and others.

Chapter 5: Fuelling Motivation with the Correct Tools

"Your talent is God's gift to you. What you do with it is your gift back to God." - Leo Buscaglia.

Nowadays and after the last big resignation (Lisa Leong, 2021) it is more important than ever to have motivated staff. Motivated staff is more productive, more creative, and more likely to stay with a company or organization. Motivating employees is crucial for unlocking their untapped potential and driving success in the workplace.

However, motivating employees is not always easy. Companies must create a work environment that fosters motivation and engagement, providing employees with the tools, resources, and opportunities they need to thrive.

The corporate world has been greatly impacted by technology. For instance, with the development of e-commerce platforms, business owners may now easily connect with clients anywhere in the world. This has given new tools and technology to people, which makes it crucial to have the abilities and information needed to use them properly. This is where programmes for education and training are quite important in this situation.

There are many things that you can do to motivate your employees, but one of the most important is to provide them with the right tools and resources.

The right tools and resources can help employees to do their jobs more effectively, which can lead to increased productivity. They can also help employees to learn and grow, which can lead to increased creativity and innovation. In addition, the right tools and resources can help to create a positive work environment, which can lead to increased employee satisfaction and engagement.

Companies who engage in employee training and development have 218% higher income per employee than those who don't, according to a survey by the (ATD, 2018) Association for Talent Development (ATD). Employees are more effective and productive when they have the right training and tools to execute their tasks.

By providing your employees with the right tools, training, and resources, you can help to motivate them and improve their performance. This can lead to increased productivity, innovation, and profitability for your company.

In this chapter, we will explore strategies for engaging and fuelling motivation in employees, from providing opportunities for growth and development to fostering a positive work environment and promoting work-life balance. By implementing these strategies, you can unlock the full potential of your team members, driving success and growth in your organization.

Leaders Role in Unlocking Unused Talent

CREATING A CULTURE of continuous improvement is not an easy task, but it is essential to ensure the success of any organization. The first step in creating a culture of continuous improvement is to establish a clear vision and mission for the organization.

This vision, mission and strategies should be communicated to all employees, so they understand the organization's purpose and goals. Once this is done, the organization needs to create a culture of constant learning, support, and growth.

This can be achieved through training, coaching, and mentoring programs that empower employees to develop their skills and knowledge.

Another important aspect of creating a culture of continuous improvement is to foster an environment of innovation and creativity.

This can be achieved by encouraging employees to come up with new ideas and solutions to problems, where all are quickly considered and implemented or put on hold until a better moment.

The organization should also provide the necessary resources and support to turn these ideas into action. Moreover, it's essential to recognise and reward employees' contributions to the organization's success, which will motivate them to continuously improve.

The modern world is packed with untapped potential, as countless individuals possess skills and abilities that have yet to be fully utilized. For many of these people, the missing ingredient in unlocking their potential is the right tools and technology. By providing individuals with access to the right tools and technology, we can unlock a vast array of untapped talent and unleash new levels of innovation and creativity.

Providing the Right Tools and Resources to Engage Talents

While Dr. Edward Deming said "85% of faults lie with systems, processes, structures and practices in an organisation and only 15% is down to operator skill and it is the responsibility of management to fix this.", we continue to find organisations that promote firefighting as a preferred mode or keep blaming the people when not having the correct systems and tools in place from the beginning.

With this rapidly changing world, it is more important than ever to have a workforce that is constantly learning and growing. By providing your employees with the right tools and resources, you can help them to stay motivated and engaged in their work.

One of my Favorite Australian slang phrases is "Running as headless chooks", which I always related to a symptom of busyness or not a state of flow. Leaders are creating this kind of environments when the right processes or tools are not provided for the best service.

There are many different tools and resources that you can provide to learn and engage your team. Some of the most important include:

- **Access to training and development opportunities**: This could include anything from formal training courses to on-the-job training. The important thing is that your employees have the opportunity to learn new skills and knowledge that will help them in their current and future roles.
- **Access to technology:** In today's world, technology is essential for learning and productivity. Make sure that your employees have access to the latest technology, such as computers, software, and mobile devices.
- **Access to information and resources**: Your employees should have easy access to the information and resources they need to do their jobs. This could include things like Business Process Maps (BPM), policies and procedures, industry news, and training materials.
- **A supportive work environment:** A caring environment is one where employees feel valued and respected. They should feel like they can ask for help when they need it and that their ideas are valued.

Fuelling Motivation to keep Engaged Talent

By providing your employees with the right tools and resources, and by creating a supportive work environment, you can help to fuel their motivation and create a culture of constant learning, support, and growth.

In addition to providing your employees with the right tools and resources, you can also help to fuel their motivation by:

- **Setting clear goals and expectations:** When employees know what is expected of them, they are more likely to be motivated to achieve those goals.
- **Providing regular feedback:** Feedback is essential for employee motivation. Make sure that you are providing your

employees with regular feedback on their performance, both positive and negative.

- **Constant Training and Growth opportunities:** When you are providing training is a good idea to keep in mind Confucius advice: "I hear and I forget. I see and I remember. I do and I understand".
- **Recognizing and rewarding success:** When employees are recognized and rewarded for their successes, they are more likely to be motivated to continue to be engaged.

In the Lean philosophy there is a very useful tool called Coaching Kata, which also acts a great motivation tool. The term "Kata" comes from martial arts and means "a series of recorded movements". The idea of the coaching Kata is to have a few predefined steps that must be completed from the current situation to a target state.

Coaching Kata can be used to fuel the motivation of your team as it includes a cross collaboration approach and breaking down the plan in simple steps. It is normally executed by asking the following 5 questions:

- What is your goal or target state?
- What is your current state?
- What obstacles are preventing you from reaching the goal state?
- What is your next step?
- When can we go and see what we have learned from taking this step?

Other practical examples of how you can keep your team engaged and growing, while providing them with the right tools and resources, include:

- **Training and development opportunities:** as mentioned in previous chapter, your team needs to have the opportunity to learn new skills and knowledge in order to stay ahead of the curve.

- **Access to mentors and coaches:** Mentors and coaches can provide employees with guidance and support as they learn and grow. Pair them up with more experienced employees to learn new skills and gain insights.
- **Access to resources and tools:** your team needs to have access to the resources and tools they need to do their jobs effectively. The latest technology includes computers, software, and mobile devices. This will help them to stay up to date on the latest trends and technologies in their field.
- **Create a library of resources:** such as books, articles, and videos. This will give them a place to go to learn new things on their own time. For example, provide customer service representatives with access to online training courses on how to handle difficult customer interactions.
- **Encourage your team to attend industry conferences and events:** This is a great way for them to network with other professionals and learn about the latest trends in their field.
- **Create a culture of feedback and recognition:** Make sure that your employees know that their contributions are valued. This will help them to feel motivated and engaged in their work. Celebrates employee successes, such as promotions, awards, and new product launches.
- **Host regular brown bag lunches:** where your team can present their ideas and get feedback from their colleagues.
- **Online tools and resources:** for example, there are many free online courses on a variety of topics, including math, tech, science, history, and economics. Some include Coursera, Udemy, LinkedIn Learning, Skillshare and even you may have already a Learning Management System (LMS) that offers online courses.

One area where technology has been particularly transformative is in the world of education. With online learning platforms, individuals can now access educational resources from anywhere in the world, allowing them to learn new skills and acquire knowledge at their own pace. This has been a game-changer for people who may have limited access to traditional educational opportunities, such as those living in rural areas or those with physical disabilities.

Another area where technology has had a major impact is in the realm of creativity. With the advent of digital tools and software, artists and designers now have access to a wide range of powerful tools that can help them bring their ideas to life. From digital painting software, AI and 3D modelling tools, these technologies have opened new avenues for expression and have allowed people to create works of art and engineering solutions that were previously unimaginable.

I hope this chapter has given you some ideas on how to provide your employees with the right tools and resources to help them learn and grow. By doing so, you can help to create a culture of constant learning, support, and growth in your organization.

Chapter Summary/Key Takeaways

- There are many things that you can do to motivate your employees, but one of the most important is to provide them with the right tools and resources.
- With this rapidly changing world, it is more important than ever to have a team that is constantly learning and growing.
- Aim to achieve a supportive work environment where your team feels valued and respected. They should feel like they can ask for help when they need it and that their ideas are valued.

Chapter 6: Let Them Glow - Embracing Flaws

"Hide not your talents. They for use were made. What's a sundial in the shade?" Benjamin Franklin

As many organizations are in the pursuit of growth and perfection, tapping into the unique skills, experiences, and perspectives of each team member is important.

However, the reality is that no individual or organization is perfect, and the fear of imperfection can be a major obstacle to success.

In this chapter, we will explore the concept of embracing imperfection and flaws in the workplace, highlighting how organizations can tap into the untapped talent of their employees by creating a culture that values learning, experimentation, and innovation.

By embracing flaws and encouraging a growth mindset, you can unlock the full potential of your workforce, driving success and achieving your goals.

The importance of embracing imperfection and flaws in the workplace

"Everybody wants to shine, but the stars don't shine, they burn", this was one of my favourite phrases from the song "All of You" in the Disney Movie Encanto. (Miranda)

While preparing this section of the book, I found a beautiful reflection on this phrase by Joel from 5Am Joel (Joel, 2022): "Most people look at stars and see perfect, beautiful, unreachable diamonds that twinkle in the sky. But in reality, stars are raging balls of fire. They're a hot mess, in a constant state of combustion and change. Being a star doesn't mean being perfect. It means embracing your flaws and dealing with your situation the best you can."

This reflection can help us drop the idea of perfectionism in the workplace, especially in a world that is changing so rapidly every day. The main intent is to learn quickly and create a mindset to reach the best outcomes for your team and customers.

The notion of embracing imperfection and flaws may seem counterintuitive. However, as I've noticed in my experience, I firmly believe that creating a culture that values learning, experimentation, and innovation is crucial for long-term success.

Embracing imperfection and flaws seems to have some great benefits such as:

- **Foster a Growth Mindset:** Embracing imperfection encourages individuals and teams to adopt a growth mindset, viewing mistakes and flaws as opportunities for learning and improvement. It shifts the focus from blame to problem-solving and personal development.
- **Drives Innovation:** A culture that values imperfection encourages employees to think creatively and take calculated risks. When individuals feel safe to explore new ideas and experiment, they are more likely to discover innovative solutions and drive organizational growth.
- **Enhances Adaptability:** In a changing business landscape, adaptability is crucial. Embracing imperfection promotes flexibility and agility, allowing you to respond quickly to changes, adjust strategies, and stay ahead of the competition.

Strategies for creating a culture that encourages experimentation and learning from failures

Pixar is a great case study of a culture that aligns key competitive advantages of creativity and quality, their production process is detail-oriented and based on constant iteration, with a team focused on growth and learning. (HBSstudent11, 2015)

According to Peter Sims article on Pixar, the former founder and president Ed Catmull "was constantly and proactively soliciting feedback from Pixar employees, who say that the mentality of constant improvement flows throughout the company."

"As with Toyota's methods, what interested Catmull the most, and appears to motivate his actions, is to constantly identify and solve new problems. When Catmull gives a public speech or lecture, what's most noticeable is that he talks about the problems that Pixar has encountered and the mistakes that he has made. Pixar has, for example, nearly burned-out its employees on numerous occasions." (Sims, 2010)

As in the Pixar example creating an environment where employees feel comfortable sharing ideas, concerns, and mistakes needs good support from the whole leadership team. They established regular channels for feedback and encouraged collaboration across different departments and hierarchical levels.

Creating an environment where employees feel safe to take risks and share their ideas without fear of judgment or punishment, needs open and honest communication, active listening, and respectful feedback.

Google is another prime example of a company that values psychological safety. They implemented initiatives such as "The Five keys to a successful Google team" which aimed to understand and enhance team effectiveness by fostering a culture of psychological safety. (ROZOVSKY, 2015)

They found five key dynamics that set successful teams apart from other teams. Here below is an extract of the 5 dynamics and questions:

- **Psychological safety:** Can we take risks on this team without feeling insecure or embarrassed?
- **Dependability:** Can we count on each other to do high quality work on time?

- **Structure & clarity:** Are goals, roles, and execution plan for our team clear?
- **Meaning of work:** Are we working on something that is personally important for each of us?
- **Impact of work:** Do we fundamentally believe that the work we're doing matters?

A great way to encourage meaning of work, experimentation and learning on your team, involves the implementation of Innovation programs, Pilot Projects, Hackathons or Prototyping events. These kinds of events encourage your teams to experiment and test new ideas and projects quickly with the Psychological Safety that are only prototypes.

This allows for iterative improvements and helps identify potential flaws early on, reducing risks associated with large-scale implementations.

The use of these strategies will need you to embrace agile methodologies like Scrum or Kanban that promote iterative development, quick feedback loops, and continuous improvement. These methodologies enable teams to experiment, learn, and adapt their approaches based on feedback and evolving requirements.

This kind of agile methodology can encourage a culture of experimentation and continuous learning through cross-functional teams and autonomous squads.

Encourage collaboration and knowledge sharing across different teams and departments. Facilitating these great opportunities for employees to work on projects outside their usual scope, will enable them to gain new perspectives and learn from colleagues' expertise.

A good example is 3M, the multinational conglomerate, that encourages cross-functional collaboration through initiatives like the "15% Rule," which allows employees to allocate a portion of their time to work on innovative projects outside their regular responsibilities. According to their website "3M's unique 15% Culture encourages employees to set aside a portion of their work time to proactively cultivate and pursue innovative ideas that excite them. While coordinating with their manager to ensure day-to-day responsibilities are still executed, employees get the space to try something new and different, think creatively and challenge the status quo". (3M's 15% Culture, n.d.)

A good thriving culture includes learning from setbacks and to achieve that you can encourage some Lessons Learned or Failure Post-Mortems sessions. After a failure or setback, you can conduct sessions to analyse the root causes, identify lessons learned, and determine process improvements.

To achieve that kind of culture, it is important to create a blame-free environment focused on learning and improvement rather than finger-pointing. For example, Pixar, the renowned animation studio, holds regular "post-mortem" meetings to analyse failures and learn from them, contributing to their culture of creativity and innovation.

Another good recommendation is to reward and recognize employees who take calculated risks, embrace experimentation, and demonstrate a commitment to learning. This can be through incentives, bonuses, or public recognition. For instance, Amazon's "Just Do It" award recognizes employees who display a bias for action and are unafraid to experiment, learn, and innovate.

Case Studies demonstrating a remarkable culture from flaws into flow

SpaceX, the aerospace manufacturer, and space transportation company founded by Elon Musk, exemplifies a culture that encourages experimentation and learning from failures. SpaceX has achieved numerous milestones in space exploration by embracing a fail-forward mentality.

They openly acknowledge and learn from their failures, using them as opportunities to iterate and improve their rocket designs. The company's iterative approach, coupled with a willingness to embrace setbacks, has enabled them to achieve remarkable successes in the space industry.

Another good case to mention is Netflix, the global streaming giant, which has fostered a culture that values experimentation and learning from failures. They encourage employees to take risks and learn from mistakes by providing them with the freedom to innovate.

One notable example is the story behind the creation of their highly successful original series, "House of Cards." Despite the traditional TV industry's reluctance to embrace such a series, Netflix took a calculated risk and released the show. Even though the series was a substantial investment, it paid off, leading to critical acclaim and widespread popularity. Netflix's culture of experimentation and learning has been instrumental in their transformation into a dominant force in the entertainment industry.

These case studies demonstrate how organizations that embrace experimentation, encourage learning from failures, and foster a culture of continuous improvement can achieve remarkable success and innovation in their respective industries.

Chapter Summary/Key Takeaways

- Creating an environment where employees feel safe to take risks and share ideas needs open and honest communication and respectful feedback.
- Creating a culture that values learning, experimentation, and innovation is crucial for long-term success.
- The main intent is to learn quickly and create a mindset to reach the best outcomes for your team and customers.

Conclusion

Unlocking the Eighth Lean Waste for success offers a compelling long-term success strategy for your organization and projects. By shifting our mindset and committing to valuing and supporting staff, we can unlock significant and far-reaching benefits.

We have reviewed together the profound impact of identifying and utilizing employee talents, leading to a more engaged, motivated, and productive teamwork.

You will be able to increase innovation, improve efficiency, and ultimately, increase profits while valuing and supporting staff with a continuous improvement culture.

Moreover, addressing the eighth Lean waste is not only about improving the bottom line, but it is also to create a positive and supportive culture that benefits both team members and your organization.

By investing in the development of internal talents, recognizing their importance, and giving time to experiment, your organizations can foster an environment that encourages growth, collaboration, and exceptional customer experience.

Going from Flaw to Flow is about harnessing the talents of our teams, knowing that despite our flaws we can align purpose with skills and abilities, providing ongoing training and development opportunities, and fostering a culture of psychological safety to unlock greater productivity, better quality, and enhanced team performance.

Hoping this guide serves you to create a supportive work environment where your team feels valued, respected, and empowered in an ever-changing business environment. Trusting that this book has sparked some ideas and suggestions to embrace open communication and provide the right tools and resources, so you can create a culture that promotes learning, experimentation, and innovation in your projects and organization.

I hope that "Flaw to Flow" has inspired you to recognize the immense value of addressing the eighth Lean waste and unleashing the potential within your organization. Now is the time to improve, act and create a culture that nurtures and harnesses the talents of your team.

I would love to hear about your experiences, challenges, and successes as you embark on this journey. Please feel free to reach out to me via email at theleanmate@outlook.com to share your insights or stay in touch to create environments where talent flourishes and innovation thrives.

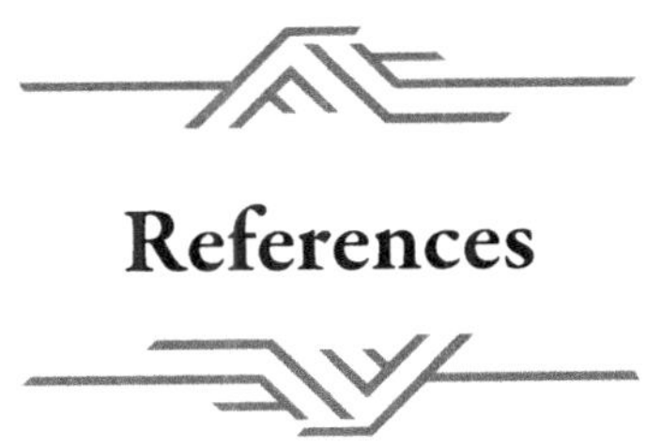

References

3M's 15% Culture. (n.d.). Retrieved from 3M's Careers: https://www.3m.co.uk/3M/en_GB/careers/culture/15-percent-culture/

ATD. (2018). *https://www.td.org*. Retrieved from New ATD Research: Investment in Talent Development on the Rise: https://www.td.org/press-release/new-atd-research-investment-in-talent-development-on-the-rise

Catalyst, N. (2016). Cultivating Great Teams: What Health Care Can Learn from Google. *NEJM Catalyst*.

Gallup. (2020). *The Relationship Between Engagement at Work and Organizational Outcomes*.

Gallup. (2022). *State of the Global Workplace Report*. Gallup.

HBSstudent11. (2015). *Pixar Animation Studios: Creative Kaizen*. Retrieved from https://d3.harvard.edu/: https://d3.harvard.edu/platform-rctom/submission/pixar-animation-studios-creative-kaizen/

James (Jim) Womack, P. (2021). *Show Respect by Exploring Problems With Your Workers*. Retrieved from https://www.lean.org/: https://www.lean.org/the-lean-post/articles/show-respect-by-exploring-problems-with-your-workers/

Joel. (2022). *Stars don't shine. They burn.* Retrieved from 5am Joel: https://5amjoel.com/stars-dont-shine-they-burn-meaning/

Linkedin. (2018). *Workplace Learning Trends.*

Lisa Leong, M. R. (2021). *Here comes the Great Resignation. Why millions of employees could quit their jobs post-pandemic.* Retrieved from https://www.abc.net.au/: https://www.abc.net.au/news/2021-09-24/the-great-resignation-post-pandemic-work-life-balance/100478866

Malikram, A. (2020). *Linkedin.* Retrieved from Leadership is not so much about technique and methods as it is about opening the heart.: https://www.linkedin.com/pulse/leadership-so-much-technique-methods-opening-heart-atul-malikram/

Miranda, L.-m. (n.d.). All Of You [Recorded by E. Movie].

PwC. (2018). *Experience is everything: here's how to get it right.* PwC. Retrieved from https://www.pwc.com/us/en/advisory-services/publications/consumer-intelligence-series/pwc-consumer-intelligence-series-customer-experience.pdf

ROZOVSKY, J. (2015). *The five keys to a successful Google team.* Retrieved from rework.withgoogle.com: https://rework.withgoogle.com/blog/five-keys-to-a-successful-google-team/

SECRETAN, L. (2004). *Inspire! What Great Leaders Do.*

Sims, P. (2010). *What Google Could Learn From Pixar*. Retrieved from Harvard Business Review: https://hbr.org/2010/08/what-google-could-learn-from-p

Sturdevant, D. (2014). *(Still) learning from Toyota*. Retrieved from McKinsey Quarterly: https://www.mckinsey.com/industries/automotive-and-assembly/our-insights/still-learning-from-toyota

Williamson, M. (n.d.). *Goodreads.com*. Retrieved from A Return to Love Quotes: https://www.goodreads.com/work/quotes/1239848-a-return-to-love-reflections-on-the-principles-of-a-course-in-miracles

Acknowledgments

Writing a book is a challenging effort, and this project would not have been possible without the support and assistance of many people. I would like to express my sincere gratitude to the following people:

First and foremost, a heartfelt thank you to all my family for their genuine support throughout this project. Their patience, encouragement, and understanding were invaluable in making this book a reality.

I would like to express my sincere gratitude to Rocio Ampie for creating such a beautiful cover for my book. Your creativity and attention to detail have made this book stand out and I am truly grateful for your hard work and dedication

I would also like to thank my colleagues and mentors along the years, who provided me guidance and expertise throughout my professional development to be able to write this book. Their insights and perspectives were instrumental in shaping its contents.

Special thanks to the editors and publishing team who worked tirelessly to bring this book to fruition. Their professionalism and attention to detail ensured the final product was of the highest quality.

Finally, I would like to express gratitude to the readers of this book, to you who have taken the time to engage with these ideas and concepts presented here. It is your curiosity and dedication that inspires me to continue exploring the world of Lean Manufacturing and business process improvement.

Thank you all for your contributions and support. This book would not have been possible without your help.

Don't miss out!

Visit the website below and you can sign up to receive emails whenever Eduardo J. Estrada publishes a new book. There's no charge and no obligation.

https://books2read.com/r/B-A-HFWX-AZXKC

BOOKS 2 READ

Connecting independent readers to independent writers.

Also by Eduardo J. Estrada

The F... Word Advantage
Sorry About the Wait
From Flaw to Flow

About the Author

Eduardo J. Estrada is an experienced Industrial Engineer with a professional background in Sustainability, Quality and Lean management. With over 15 years of experience, the author has worked extensively in the manufacturing industry, identifying, and implementing process improvements to enhance efficiency and reduce waste.

The author has been recognized for his contributions to sustainability and operations excellence, having been instrumental in winning awards for the companies where he has worked. Currently residing in Australia with his family, the author enjoys spending his free time travelling, cycling, reading, and working on improving business processes.

With a passion for continuous improvement and a deep understanding of Lean Manufacturing tools, the author brings a wealth of knowledge and expertise to this book. Through his work, the author aims to help organizations reduce wait times and queues, improve customer experience, and drive business success.

If you want to learn more about these topics or would like to start a conversation, you can reach out at: theleanmate@outlook.com